THE BOOK OF WHO?

W9-BXZ-184

KINGFISHER
NEW YORK

KINGFISHER
LONDON & NEW YORK

Copyright © Kingfisher 2010
Published in the United States by Kingfisher,
175 Fifth Ave., New York, NY 10010
Kingfisher is an imprint of Macmillan Children's Books, London.

Illustrated by Del Frost
Concept by Jo Connor

Distributed in the U.S. by Macmillan, 175 Fifth Ave.,
New York, NY 10010
Distributed in Canada by H.B. Fenn and Company Ltd.,
34 Nixon Road, Bolton, Ontario L7E 1W2

Library of Congress Cataloging-in-Publication data has
been applied for.

ISBN: 978-0-7534-6418-2

Kingfisher books are available for special
promotions and premiums. For details contact:
Special Markets Department, Macmillan,
175 Fifth Avenue, New York, NY 10010.

For more information, please visit
www.kingfisherbooks.com

Printed in China
10 9 8 7 6 5 4 3 2 1
1TR/0510/LFG/UNTD/140MA

WHAT'S IN THIS BOOK?

WHO OR WHOSE..

HAVE YOU EVER ASKED YOURSELF WHO?

It's only natural to be confused by the world around us . . . It is a very complicated and surprising place sometimes! And you'll never understand what's going on around you unless you ask yourself "WHO?" every now and then.

"Who" is what this book is all about.

We have traveled over the land, under the sea, up mountains, across deserts—and even into outer space—to collect as many tricky questions as we could find . . .

. . . and we also found the answers for you!

We now invite you to come with us on our journey around the world of "WHO" so that we can show you all the answers we have discovered.

Did you know . . .

An emperor penguin can hold its breath for 20 minutes when diving for fish.

While we were searching for all those answers, we found out some other pretty interesting things, too. We wrote them all down on these panels—so you can memorize these facts and impress your friends!

We also thought it might be fun to see how much of this shiny new knowledge you can remember—so at the back of the book, on pages 56 and 57, you'll find some Quick-Quiz questions to test you. It's not as scary as it sounds—we promise it'll be fun. (And besides, we've given you all the answers on pages 58 and 59.)

Are you ready for this big adventure? Then let's go!

QUICK-QUIZ QUESTIONS

WHO WERE THE FIRST EXPLORERS?

Some of the earliest ocean voyages were made by the Polynesian peoples of New Guinea. Almost 3,500 years ago, they began leaving their homeland to explore the vast Pacific Ocean in nothing bigger than canoes.

Did you know . . .

Polynesians were not just great explorers—they were also very artistic. Their designs and jewelry are still popular today.

WHO WENT TO SEA IN JUNKS?

Junks are Chinese sailing ships. One of the greatest Chinese explorers was Zheng He. By the early 1400s, his junk ships were the world's biggest and were five times the size of European ships.

Did you know . . .

Zheng He's fleet of junks sailed as far as East Africa, and they traveled back with a giraffe!

7

WHOSE JOURNEY LASTED 24 YEARS?

Arab explorer Ibn Battuta's adventures began in 1325, when he set out from his hometown of Tangier, Morocco. He was so bitten by the travel bug that he didn't return home until 1349!

Did you know . . .

Ibn Battuta wrote a book about his travels, but his memory was not always that good. He said he had seen hippos with horselike heads and that the Egyptian pyramids were cone shaped!

WHO RAN THE FIRST MARATHON?

In 490 B.C., the ancient Greeks won a battle at Marathon, about 25 miles (40 kilometers) from Athens. A Greek soldier named Pheidippides ran all the way to Athens to tell the citizens the good news. He was so exhausted from running that he collapsed and died.

Did you know . . .

Marathon races today are 26 miles (42 kilometers) long. They were changed from 25 miles (40 kilometers) at the 1908 Olympic Games, held in London, England.

WHO WERE THE CONQUISTADORS?

When Christopher Columbus discovered the Americas, rumors spread that they were rich in gold. Spanish soldiers began heading there in search of their fortunes. The soldiers were known as conquistadors, from the Spanish word for "conqueror," because they were more interested in conquering new lands (and their riches) than exploring them.

Did you know . . .

The native peoples of the Americas did not use gold as money. Instead, they valued it for its beauty.

WHO WERE THE ANCIENT GREEKS?

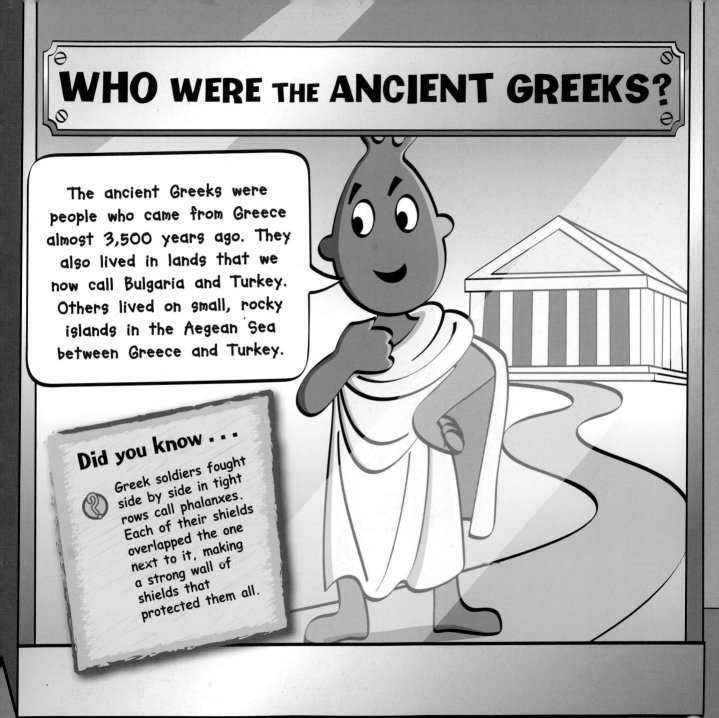

The ancient Greeks were people who came from Greece almost 3,500 years ago. They also lived in lands that we now call Bulgaria and Turkey. Others lived on small, rocky islands in the Aegean Sea between Greece and Turkey.

Did you know . . .

Greek soldiers fought side by side in tight rows call phalanxes. Each of their shields overlapped the one next to it, making a strong wall of shields that protected them all.

WHO FIRST SAILED AROUND THE WORLD?

A Portuguese explorer named Ferdinand Magellan led the first expedition that sailed around the world, in 1519–1522. He set sail from Spain with five ships and 270 crew members. Magellan was killed during a battle, and only one ship returned, carrying 18 men.

Did you know . . .

While sailing around the Americas, Magellan and his crew ran out of food. They ate rats, leather, and sawdust to stop themselves from starving.

WHO HAD HIS BEST IDEAS IN THE BATHTUB?

Archimedes was a mathematician who lived in Greece around 250 B.C. and invented many things, including the catapult. He is famous for shouting "Eureka!" after having solved a problem he was thinking about while taking a bath.

Did you know . . .

One famous Greek thinker was Digenes. He lived in an old wooden barrel, so people could see he didn't care about money or possessions.

WHO SOLVED THE PUZZLE OF THE LONGEST RIVER?

Until the 1860s, Europeans had no idea where the Nile, the world's longest river, began. Then British explorer John Hanning Speke proved that it flowed out of the vast African lake today known as Lake Victoria.

Did you know...

The Nile River is approximately 4,160 miles (6,695 kilometers) long and flows through as many as ten countries in Africa.

WHO WORKED TO A BEAT?

Rowers on Greek warships worked in time to the music of a drummer or piper. The beat kept the oars moving together and stopped them from getting tangled up.

Did you know . . .

Your heart beats about 90 times every minute. But when you listen to fast-paced music, your heart rate speeds up.

WHO DISCOVERED THAT EARTH IS ROUND?

Did you know . . .

There are two types of eclipses. A lunar eclipse is when Earth moves between the Sun and the Moon. A solar eclipse is when the Moon moves between Earth and the Sun, blocking the Sun's light.

In about 470 B.C., a Greek scientist named Parmenides was watching an eclipse of the Moon. He noticed that Earth cast a dark shadow on the Moon and figured out that if the shadow was curved, Earth must be round.

WHO WERE THE FIRST PEOPLE IN SPACE?

Did you know . . .

The first people to walk on the Moon were Americans Neil Armstrong and Edwin "Buzz" Aldrin in July 1969.

Russian cosmonaut Yuri Gagarin was the first person ever to travel into space, in April 1961. The first woman to get liftoff was also a Russian—Valentina Tereshkova circled Earth for almost three days in June 1963.

17

WHO TURNED OFF THE RAIN?

A drought can occur when not enough rain falls. This means there is very little drinking water and it is difficult to grow crops. Since the 1970s, the number of serious droughts around the world has doubled.

WHO STARTED TALKING?

Nobody knows how or when people first spoke. They might have started by copying sounds around them, such as the whistling of the wind. By communicating with words, humans could more easily help one another.

Did you know . . .

There are more than 6,900 living languages. The language with the greatest number of speakers is Mandarin Chinese, with more than one billion speakers!

WHO SENT THE FIRST RADIO BROADCAST?

The first true radio set that sent messages using radio waves was built by Italian inventor Guglielmo Marconi. But he was not the first person to prove the existence of radio waves—that was German scientist Heinrich Hertz.

Did you know . . .

 Radio waves can be almost as long as a football field—about 330 feet (100 meters)!

WHO WROTE IN SECRET CODE?

In medieval times, Scandinavians and Anglo-Saxons sometimes wrote using runes, which were drawn with straight lines. The word *rune* means "secret." Few people could read or write 1,000 years ago. Some thought that anyone who could understand the runes must have magical powers!

Did you know . . .

The ancient Egyptians used the stalks of papyrus plants to make paper. The word *paper* comes from *papyrus*.

WHO WRITES WITH A PAINTBRUSH?

Did you know . . .

There are about 50,000 Chinese symbols. Schoolchildren have to learn only about 5,000 of them, though.

In China and Japan, people sometimes paint words as symbols, slowly and beautifully, using a brush and ink. The art of beautiful handwriting is called calligraphy. Japanese children learn calligraphy in school.

WHO CAN TELL TIME WITHOUT A CLOCK?

Inside every one of us there's something called a body clock. It wakes us up every morning and tells us it's breakfast time. And all through the day we seem to know just when it's time to work, eat, and play. As evening comes, we feel tired and get ready to sleep.

Did you know . . .

Some animals sleep through the day and come out only at night. This is called nocturnal behavior. A badger is a nocturnal animal.

WHO TOOK HOURS TO TAKE A PICTURE?

Cliccccccck!

A Frenchman named Joseph Niépce took the first photograph in 1826. He had to wait eight hours before the picture was captured on a thin metal plate coated with a kind of tar. The photograph showed the view from his window.

Did you know . . .

The first photograph was of farm buildings and the sky. Niépce called it a heliograph, after the Greek word for the Sun—*helios*.

WHO INVENTED OUR CALENDAR?

More than 2,000 years ago, a Roman ruler named Julius Caesar invented the calendar that we use today. He gave each year 365 days and arranged the days into 12 months. Since then, the calendar has hardly changed.

Did you know...

The names of our months are taken from the names of Roman gods and rulers. July is named after Julius Caesar.

SUN	MON	TUE
1	2	3
8	9	10

WHO WERE THE ROMANS?

Did you know . . .

It would have taken almost 100 days to ride from one end of the Roman Empire to the other. It was a journey of more than 3,000 Roman miles—around 2,800 miles (4,500 kilometers) today.

The Romans were people who came from Rome. About 2,000 years ago, they became so powerful that they began to conquer the lands around them. By A.D. 100, they ruled a huge empire and were one of the mightiest peoples in the ancient world.

WHO RULED ROME?

Over the years, Rome was ruled in three different ways: first by kings, then by a number of officials who were chosen by the people, and finally by an emperor—a ruler with great power and rank.

The king of Egypt was called the pharaoh. The Egyptians believed that their Sun god Ra was the first king of Egypt and that all of the pharaohs after him were his relatives. This made the pharaoh very holy—and very powerful! The people thought the pharaoh was a god on Earth.

Did you know...

Hatshepsut was a famous female pharaoh. She had to wear badges of royalty, including a false beard made of real hair.

29

WHOSE FEET KEEP AN EGG WARM?

Every year, in the middle of the winter in Antarctica, a female emperor penguin lays one egg and gives it to her mate to keep warm. He balances the egg between his feet and his feathers until it is ready to hatch in the early spring.

Did you know . . .

 An emperor penguin can hold its breath for 20 minutes when diving for fish.

WHO IS THE BEST-DRESSED BIRD?

Male birds of paradise grow beautiful feathers during the breeding season. When a female comes by, all the males hang upside down to show off their stunning plumage. It is a beauty contest, and the female picks the bird with the finest feathers to be her mate.

Did you know . . .

The male palm cockatoo attracts a mate by playing a drumbeat. It grasps a twig in one foot and beats it against a log.

WHO IS AT HOME IN A BUBBLE?

Baby froghoppers are often called spittlebugs because they make a bubbly froth very soon after they are born. They hide in this "cuckoo spit" while they feed and grow.

Did you know . . .

Spittlebugs can jump up to 100 times their body length!

WHO STARTS LIFE WITH A JUMP?

Mallard ducks often nest in holes in trees, so their ducklings hatch high up above the ground. When their mother calls, they jump out and tumble to the ground. They are so light that they all land safe and sound.

Did you know . . .

There are more mallard ducks on Earth than any other type of duck.

WHOSE TONGUE IS LONGER THAN ITS TAIL?

The chameleon's sticky-tipped tongue is not just longer than its tail—it is longer than its whole body! The lizard shoots it out very quickly and reels back a tasty bug.

Did you know...

 Many lizards can snap off their tails when they're being attacked. A new tail grows back after a few weeks.

WHOSE HORSE HAD EIGHT LEGS?

The Vikings called their chief god Odin. They believed he rode an eight-legged horse called Sleipnir that could gallop across land, sea, and sky.

WHOSE HOUSE IS A TRAPDOOR?

The trapdoor spider's burrow has a door with a silk hinge that can open and close. The spider hides inside, waiting for passing insects. When it hears one, it flings open the trapdoor and grabs its victim.

Did you know . . .

All spiders can spin silk, but they do not all make webs. The spitting spider catches insects by spitting a sticky gum over them.

There are 1,000 species of paper wasps worldwide, with many living in Australia and North America.

WHOSE HOUSE IS PAPER THIN?

The paper wasp's nest has paper walls. It makes the paper by chewing up strips of wood that it tears from plants or old fence posts. It spreads the mixture in thin layers to build a nest.

WHO WORE STEEPLES ON THEIR HEADS?

All kinds of weird and wonderful headdresses passed in and out of fashion in Europe during the Middle Ages. In the 1400s, women began wearing tall hats called hennins, which looked a lot like church steeples. Some hennins were almost 3 ft. (1m) high!

Did you know...

The hats in the Middle Ages were sometimes shaped like part of an animal. Some were shaped like animals' horns and others like butterflies' wings.

Did you know . . .

Women are not allowed to visit Mount Athos— the "holy mountain" —in Greece. Even female animals are banned!

WHO WERE THE MOUNTAIN MEN?

American explorers such as Kit Carson became known as mountain men during the 1800s. They roamed through the wildest parts of the Rocky Mountains, trapping beavers and other animals for their fur.

WHO WAS JOAN OF ARC?

Joan was a French peasant girl who grew up when England and France were at war. In 1429, at the age of 17, she dressed up as a soldier and helped free the city of Orléans from an English army. But a year later, she was captured and burned at the stake.

Did you know . . .

Joan of Arc is the youngest person in history to command a nation's army.

Temujin was the son of a leader of the Mongol people of central Asia. He was born in 1162, and he became a warrior when he was only 13, after his father died. Temujin took the name Genghis Khan. Under his leadership, the Mongols attacked and won many lands in Asia.

Did you know · · ·

In the early 1200s, the Mongol Empire covered 2 percent of Earth and had a population of 100 million.

WHO RIDES A BUCKING BRONCO?

Did you know . . .

 Another rodeo event is steer roping. A cowhand gallops after a steer (male bull) and tries to catch it with a lasso.

Cowhands ride in competitions called rodeos. A bronco is an untamed horse, and cowhands test their riding skills by trying to stay on a bronco's back for a few seconds—bareback or with a saddle.

WHO TELLS STORIES BY DANCING?

Ballet is a way of telling a story through music and dance. The sound of the music and the movements of the dancers tell you what's going on as clearly as any story in a book.

43

WHO LIVES IN THE RAINFOREST?

Did you know . . .

Few tribal children go to school. Their parents teach them how to survive in the rainforest.

Many different tribes live in the world's rainforests. Most build homes and dig vegetable gardens where they grow their own food. The soil in rainforests is poor, however, and the tribes are unable to grow food year after year. After a while, the tribes pack up and move on to another part of the forest.

44

WHO WERE "WISE" HUMANS?

Did you know . . .

The first humanlike creatures lived about 4.5 million years ago. They were called *Australopithecus*.

Modern humans are intelligent, which is why our scientific name is Homo sapiens, meaning "wise human." The first Homo sapiens evolved in Africa almost 200,000 years ago.

WHO BUILT PALACES IN THE MOUNTAINS?

Back in the 1400s, the Inca ruled over vast parts of the Andes Mountains in South America. They built amazing stone towns and palaces in the mountains, including the mysterious Machu Picchu.

Did you know . . .

The site Machu Picchu had been deserted for more than 400 years, until American explorer Hiram Bingham rediscovered it in 1911.

WHO ARE THE GREATEST TUNNELERS?

At the moment, the greatest tunnel builders are the Japanese. Their 33.4-mi.- (53.8-km-) long Seikan railroad tunnel links the Honshu and Hokkaido islands. In 2017, the Swiss Gotthard Base Tunnel under the Alps will open. It will be an amazing 35.4 mi. (57.1km) long.

Did you know . . .

From planning to opening, the Seikan railroad tunnel took 42 years to construct.

WHO FIRST FLUSHED THE TOILET?

Almost 400 years ago, Sir John Harrington, built a flushing toilet for his godmother, Queen Elizabeth I of England. In those days, very few homes had water pipes or drains, so ordinary people had to use chamber pots.

WHO FIRST TOOK A BATH?

Did you know . . .

Almost 500 years ago, the Chinese used pigs' hair to make the first toothbrushes!

In ancient times, the people of Greece, Rome, and the Indus Valley in Pakistan enjoyed taking baths. But, as time went by, baths went out of fashion, and many people never even washed. They used perfumes to cover up the smell!

WHO USED TEA AS MONEY?

Did you know . . .

The Chinese first used paper money about 1,200 years ago. They printed some of the money on the bark of mulberry trees.

People in Tibet and China once used tea pressed into blocks as money. Before coins were invented, people used to swap things like shells, beads, and grain for the goods they wanted.

WHO COPIED THE GREEKS?

About 2,000 years ago, the Romans marched into Greece. They conquered its armies and added its lands to their own empire. But Roman people respected the Greek ways of life. They admired Greek poetry, plays, buildings, and art. They copied many Greek ideas and used them to improve their own ways of life.

Did you know . . .

There were more than 40 religious holidays in Athens each year. There are paintings of these festivals on Greek pottery and wine jars.

WHO WERE THE FIRST FARMERS?

Did you know . . .

The first crops were wheat and barley, and the first farm animals were goats and sheep.

1ST

2ND

Farming began about 10,000 years ago, when people in the Middle East began saving the seeds of wild plants to sow as their own crops. Growing their own food meant that farmers could stay in the same place all year long.

WHO READS FROM RIGHT TO LEFT?

To read a book in Arabic or Hebrew, you have to work from right to left. So if this book were in Arabic, the first page would be where the "farewell" is now.

Did you know . . .

The oldest printed book in the world is believed to be *The Diamond Sutra*, which dates from A.D. 868.

WHOSE SINGING WRECKED SHIPS?

In fairy tales, mermaids were magical creatures—half women and half fish—who lived in the ocean near dangerous, rocky coasts. They sang so sweetly that the sailors who heard them forgot everything else—including how to steer their ships away from the rocks!

Did you know...

The patron saint of music is Saint Cecilia. In pictures of her, she usually has a miniature organ on her lap.

WHO SINGS UNDERWATER?

Did you know . . .

Humpback whale calves do not stop growing until they are ten years old.

Humpback whales seem to sing to one another under the ocean. It is thought that they are singing to attract a mate. No other animal's song lasts as long as the humpback's, and it can be heard hundreds of miles away.

QUICK-QUIZ QUESTIONS

1. Which ocean did Polynesian peoples explore almost 3,500 years ago?

2. How many miles is a modern marathon?

3. Which language does the word conquistador come from?

4. Where did the Greek thinker Diogenes live?

5. Where does the Nile River begin?

6. Name the two types of eclipses that can occur.

7. What is a drought?

8. Which language has the greatest number of speakers?

9. Unscramble ALL CHIP GRAY to spell the art of beautiful writing.

10. What does the Greek word *helios* mean?

11. The month of July is named after which Roman ruler?

12. Hatshepsut was a famous male pharaoh. True or false?

13. Where do emperor penguins live?

14. What is another name for a froghopper?

15. Unscramble OCEAN HELM to spell the name of a sticky-tongued lizard.

16. All spiders can spin silk. True or false?

17. What is the name for a tall hat worn by women in the 1400s?

18. How old was Temujin (Genghis Khan) when he became a warrior?

19. In which competitions do cowhands take part?

20. What is the scientific name for modern humans?

21. Which mountain range is home to the Inca site Machu Picchu?

22. What did the Chinese use to make the first toothbrushes?

23. What items were once used by people in Tibet and China to buy goods?

24. Which languages read from right to left?

25. Which whale's song can travel many miles?

QUICK-QUIZ ANSWERS

1. The Pacific Ocean.

2. A modern marathon is 26 miles (42 kilometers).

3. Spanish.

4. In a barrel.

5. It flows out of Lake Victoria, in Africa.

6. Lunar and solar eclipses.

7. A drought is a severe shortage of rainfall.

8. Mandarin Chinese, with more than one billion speakers.

9. ALL CHIP GRAY = calligraphy.

10. The Sun.

11. Julius Caesar.

12. False. Hatshepsut was female.

13. In Antarctica.

14. A spittlebug.

15. OCEAN HELM = chameleon.

16. True.

17. A hennin.

18. He was 13 years old.

19. Rodeos.

20. Homo sapiens.

21. The Andes Mountains in South America.

22. Pigs' hair.

23. Tea, shells, beads, and grain.

24. Arabic and Hebrew.

25. The humpback whale's.

TRICKY WORDS

ANGLO-SAXONS
People who lived in England from the
A.D. 400s to 1066.

ANTARCTICA
Earth's icy, southernmost
area around the South Pole.

BREEDING SEASON
The time when male and female animals
come together to produce offspring.

BROADCAST
To send out a program over radio
waves so that it can be heard on a
radio or watched on a television.
A program sent this way is also
called a broadcast.

CATAPULT
A weapon that is used
to throw something, such
as a rock, quickly through
the air.

CITIZENS
The people who live in
a particular area, such
as a town, city, or country.

COMMUNICATING
Sharing information with someone,
such as by speaking or writing.

CONQUER
To win and take control of something.

COSMONAUT
The Russian word for an astronaut.
An astronaut is a person who travels
into space to find out more about it.

CROPS
Plants, such as wheat, corn,
or potatoes, that are grown over
large areas in fields for food.

DROUGHT
A long period of time in which no rain falls.
Rivers can dry up and plants can die without
water. Food and drinking water may be hard
to find in areas suffering from drought.

EMPIRE
A large area of land, usually several countries,
ruled by one government. The Romans had a
huge empire.

EXPEDITION
An organized journey, such as one in which
people travel to explore part of a country.

FLEET
A group of ships sailing together.

INCA
People who lived from 700 to
450 years ago in South America.
The center of their empire was in Peru.

INVENTOR
A person who is the first to think of
or create something.

LASSO
A long rope with a loop at one end. It is thrown so that the loop falls around an animal's neck.

LUNAR
Describes something that involves the Moon.

MAJOR
Describes something that is important or serious.

MIDDLE AGES
The period in Europe between A.D. 476 and 1500. These years are also called the medieval period.

NATIVE PEOPLE
The first people who originally lived in a country, before settlers arrived from other countries.

NOCTURNAL
Describes something that happens at night. Nocturnal animals are active at night.

OLYMPIC GAMES
First begun in ancient Greece, the Olympic Games are sporting events that take place every four years. Athletes from all over the world take part to win gold, silver, or bronze medals.

POSSESSIONS
Objects that are owned.

PYRAMID
A large, stone building with four triangular sides. Pyramids were built as tombs for ancient Egyptian kings and queens, who were buried with all of their riches.

RANK
A person's position in a group, such as in an army.

ROMANS
Ancient people from Italy who lived around 2,000 years ago in Europe, Africa, and Asia.

SCANDINAVIA
A region in northern Europe that includes Denmark, Norway, and Sweden.

SILK
Fine threads that are made by insects and woven together to make a soft, smooth, and strong material.

SOLAR
Describes something that involves the Sun.

SYMBOL
A shape or design that is drawn to show an idea of something, such as a word.

TAR
A black, sticky substance that comes from rocks. Tar is used to coat the surface of roads.

VIKINGS
People from Scandinavia who sailed and battled with other people in the world, especially in northeastern Europe, from the A.D. 700s to the 1000s.

WHERE TO FIND STUFF

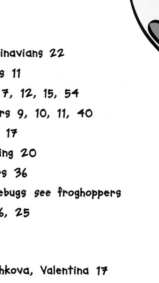

Wow! What an amazing journey! We hope you had as much fun as we did and learned many new things. Who knew there was so much to discover about "who"! Speaking of "who," we can tell you that we'll soon be going on a few more exciting journeys:

The Book of . . . Why?
The Book of . . . What?
The Book of . . . How?

Look out for these great books!
"Who" knows "what" we'll discover . . .

See you soon!